211 Powerful Night Prayers that Will Take Your Life to the Next Level:

Powerful Prayers & Declarations for Deliverance, Healing, Breakthrough & Release of Your Detained Blessings

MOSES OMOJOLA

ISBN-10: 1981478922
ISBN-13: 978-1981478927

DEDICATION

To God Almighty.

CONTENTS

ACKNOWLEDGMENTS

I acknowledged all those who made this work a success.

Preface

Every man on planet earth desires to be successful, becomes wealthy and enjoy divine health, with money being able to answer to every of his need at every point in time. However, unpleasant powers from Satan tend to hinder the manifestation of this wishful ambition, make it a mirage, and cause many to wonder why financial lack and other vices stir them on the face! You might have used all known ways you can use to become successful and live happily to no avail, and felt time is fast running out. This is why this book of prayers has been divinely orchestrated your way in this time of immense need.

This book contains over 211 special Prayers that will give you victory over Satan and his agents, and connect you to success and breakthroughs quickly, when you pray the prayers in this book zealously. These prayers are systematically and spiritually arranged to give you the much needed help.

Chapter 1

Prayers for Release of Detained Blessings

PRAYER: O Lord, give me great intelligence that will trouble my accusers, in the name of Jesus.

PRAYER: O Lord, let water of blessings from your altar, enter into my life, in the name of Jesus.

PRAYER: Every evil spoke against my life, be cancelled, in the name of Jesus.

PRAYER: Like Abraham, Isaac, Jacob and Joseph, O Lord, make me to be exceedingly rich, in the name of Jesus.

PRAYER: Father Lord, put my matter in heart of kings, let them shower me with honor and promotion, in the name of Jesus.

PRAYER: Anywhere my blessings are buried, angels of deliverance, locate them and uproot them tonight, in the name of Jesus.

PRAYER: O Lord, let me not lack any good thing, in the name of Jesus.

PRAYER: O Lord, Like the biblical Lot, make me to be very wealth, in the name of Jesus.

PRAYER: You cloud of darkness attacking my breakthroughs, disappear fire, in the name of Jesus.

PRAYER: Father Lord, trouble my helpers spirits as you did to King Ahasuerus, let them know no peace until they bless me as you have commanded them, in the name of Jesus.

PRAYER: Every altar frustrating my life, release me and scatter, in the name of Jesus.

PRAYER: Lord, direct your plague to the camps of my enemies, in the name of Jesus.

PRAYER: Every yoke of limitation in my life, break, in the name of Jesus.

PRAYER: Every demonic gang up against my life, scatter now, in the name of Jesus.

PRAYER: You my blessings from the north, south, east and west, manifest by speedily, in the name of Jesus.

PRAYER: Exceeding wealth is my portion, in the name of Jesus.

PRAYER: I receive celestial wisdom to multiply my income, in the name of Jesus.

PRAYER: Every power fuelling trouble in my life, die, in the name of Jesus.

PRAYER: Any evil mark releasing frustration into my life, be wiped off by the blood of Jesus.

PRAYER: I claim divine health, in the name of Jesus.

PRAYER: Today, I come out from every wilderness of hardship, in the name of Jesus.

PRAYER: Every occultic pronouncement against my life, be nullified, in the name of Jesus.

PRAYER: O Lord, let every blessing you have released into my life in the spirit realm, manifest speedily in the physical, in the name of Jesus.

PRAYER: You my household enemies, scatter by fire, in the name of Jesus.

PRAYER: Every unfriendly friend in my life, be exposed and be disconnected, in the name of Jesus.

PRAYER: Tonight, O Lord, let every promise you have made concerning my life, manifest, in the name of Jesus.

PRAYER: Every yoke limiting my blessings, break, in the name of Jesus.

PRAYER: O Lord, let my greatness, come alive, in the name of Jesus.

PRAYER: Father Lord, let every power that curse me receive its curse back, in the name of Jesus.

PRAYER: You mark of hatred in me, be wiped off by the blood of Jesus.

PRAYER: Yoke of hatred placed upon my life, break now, in the name of Jesus.

PRAYER: O Lord, baptize me now with anointing of prosperity, in the name of Jesus.

PRAYER: Father Lord, let your blessings manifest in my life to affect my generation, in the name of Jesus.

PRAYER: I receive divine authority to possess my possession, in the name of Jesus.

PRAYER: Every fountain of lack in my life, dry up, in the name of Jesus.

PRAYER: Every fountain of anger in my life, dry up, in the name of Jesus.

PRAYER: Any channel of affliction into my life, be blocked with the hand of God, in the name of Jesus.

PRAYER: Every yoke of satanic delay in any area of my life, I command you to break, in the name of Jesus.

PRAYER: Spirit of disobedience ruling my life, I bind you, in the name of Jesus.

PRAYER: Every garment of affliction wore upon my life, be removed now, in the name of Jesus.

PRAYER: O Lord, release your troubles upon those that trouble me, in the name of Jesus.

PRAYER: Every cord of backwardness in my life and business, be cut off by the sword of God.

Chapter 2
Prayers for Divine Favor

PRAYER: Father Lord, let my good speak for me in time of affliction and oppression, in the name of Jesus.

PRAYER: You seed of hatred in me, die, in the name of Jesus.

PRAYER: Every spirit of rejection dragging my life backward, I bind you, in the name of Jesus.

PRAYER: Every anti-success foundation fashioned against my life, I pull you down, in the name of Jesus.

PRAYER: You unfriendly friend in my life, be disgraced now, in the name of Jesus.

PRAYER: Angels of God, ascend and descend and released my blessings to me, in the name of Jesus.

PRAYER: O Lord, scatter the wasters, in the name of Jesus.

PRAYER: Spirit of emptiers assigned against my life, I bind you, in the name of Jesus.

PRAYER: You spirit of wasters wasting my life and efforts, be terminated, in the name of Jesus.

PRAYER: Any power anywhere attacking my resources, wherever you are, be expired, in the name of Jesus.

PRAYER: O Lord, let anointing for divine restoration, manifest in my life, in the name of Jesus.

PRAYER: O Lord, let my hands minister to my needs and that of my family, in the name of Jesus.

PRAYER: Fire of deliverance, enter the camp of my enemies and scatter their plans and give me victory, in the name of Jesus.

PRAYER: Anointing for signs and wonder, locate me by fire, in the name of Jesus.

PRAYER: Anointing that cannot be disgraced or insulted, come upon my life, in the name of Jesus.

PRAYER: Sword of vengeance, visit the camp of my

enemies and scatter their habitation, in the name of Jesus.

A Call For Short Review On Amazon

Enjoying this book so far or receiving value from it in anyway? Then, I would like to ask you for a favor: kindly post a quick review for this book on its Amazon page.

When you get to the book page on Amazon, gently scroll down the page till you reach **"Write A Customer Review"** and click on it.

Kindly Click Here to Write the Review Now

PRAYER: O Lord, take me to my promise land, in the name of Jesus.

PRAYER: Every bitterness in my life, be removed now, in the name of Jesus.

PRAYER: Let the wickedness of the wicked, come to an end, in the name of Jesus.

PRAYER: Every spirit bewitching my life, be arrested, in the name of Jesus.

PRAYER: Lord, let my enemies be rendered impotent, in the name of Jesus.

PRAYER: Spirit of barrenness in my life, business and marriage, I bind you, in the name of Jesus.

PRAYER: Every evil attachment existing in my life, be removed by fire, in the name of Jesus.

PRAYER: Every cry of the aggrieved over my life, be silenced now, in the name of Jesus.

PRAYER: I receive strength to live a Holy life and affect my generation positively, in the name of Jesus.

PRAYER: You that wicked power luring me to sin,

die, in the name of Jesus.

PRAYER: Exceeding abundance, manifest in my life with divine proofs now, in the name of Jesus.

PRAYER: Every demonic altar erected against my life, be uprooted, in the name of Jesus.

PRAYER: You demonic strongman attacking my fruitfulness, be disgraced by fire, in the name of Jesus.

PRAYER: I receive uncommon favor and blessings in the name of Jesus.

PRAYER: O Lord, let your spoken miracles concerning my life manifest now, in the name of Jesus.

PRAYER: You my blessings in heavenly places, manifest spiritually now, in the name of Jesus.

PRAYER: You my hanging blessings, come alive, in the name of Jesus.

PRAYER: Anointing for fruitfulness and multiplication locate me today, in the name of Jesus.

PRAYER: You my inheritance, come alive by fire, in

the name of Jesus.

PRAYER: Arrow of shame and disgrace from the kingdom of darkness, go back to your sender, in the name of Jesus.

PRAYER: Holy spirit decree my fruitfulness now, in the name of Jesus.

PRAYER: O Lord, let my life be filled with testimonies continually, in the name of Jesus.

PRAYER: Father Lord, let my well of life be replenished, in the name of Jesus.

PRAYER: Holy Ghost, help me to pray answered prayers, in the name of Jesus.

PRAYER: The grace to know the mind of Christ in every matter before me, and take the right decisions, fall upon my life, in the name of Jesus.

PRAYER: Trumpet of victory and promotion, blow in my favor, in the name of Jesus.

PRAYER:, O Lord, let me understand the time and season, what I should do to succeed in all endeavor like the children of Isaachar, in the name of Jesus.

PRAYER: You that power attacking my finances, die, in the name of Jesus.

PRAYER: O lord, set me free from every affliction, in the name of Jesus.

PRAYER: Any power anywhere holding my life captive, receive the judgment of God, in the name of Jesus.

PRAYER: I receive uncommon anointing to live a fulfilling life, in the name of Jesus.

PRAYER: My set time of favor shall not be thwarted, in the name of Jesus.

Chapter 3

Prayers to Possess your Possession

PRAYER: O Lord, destroy the power house of my enemies, in the name of Jesus.

PRAYER: Every counsel against my life likened to the counsel of Ahitophel, be terminated, in the name of Jesus.

PRAYER: Father Lord, put spiritual demarcation between me and my arch enemies, in the name of Jesus.

PRAYER: Divine wisdom to handle money, I receive you, in the name of Jesus.

PRAYER: You devouring spirit, I bind you, in the name of Jesus.

PRAYER: O Lord, bless my water and my bread, in the name of Jesus.

PRAYER: Any evil hand stretched against my life, business and family, wither, in the name of Jesus.

PRAYER: Father Lord, decorate my life with beauty, in the name of Jesus.

PRAYER: Every seed of bitterness in my life, I command you to dry up, in the name of Jesus.

PRAYER: Today O Lord, do marvelous things in my life, in the name of Jesus.

PRAYER: I shall prosper in whatever thing I do, in the name of Jesus.

PRAYER: You that power employed to waste my effort, die, in the name of Jesus.

PRAYER: O Lord, promote me from glory to glory, in the name of Jesus.

PRAYER: Every evil tree in my foundation, wither, in the name of Jesus.

PRAYER: Success that knows no limit, locate me now, in the name of Jesus.

PRAYER: O Lord, give me divine direction at every point in life, in the name of Jesus.

PRAYER: You that power ministering confusion into my life, be destroyed, in the name of Jesus.

PRAYER: Tonight O Lord, order my step to my place of prosperity, in the name of Jesus.

PRAYER: Spirit of delay and procrastination, be frustrated, in the name of Jesus.

PRAYER: You arrow of sickness fashioned against my life, return to your sender, in the name of Jesus.

PRAYER: You evil seed destroying my life, be flushed out, by the blood of Jesus.

PRAYER: Every monitoring spirit monitoring my life for destruction, I bind you, in the name of Jesus.

PRAYER: Let every demonic projection be dislodged, in the name of Jesus.

PRAYER: Angels of blessing, locate me now, in the name of Jesus.

PRAYER: Angel Gabriel, pay me special visitation and release the Lord blessings to me, in the name of Jesus.

PRAYER: I shall not die but live and fulfill my destiny, in the name of Jesus.

PRAYER: Every manipulation in the kingdom of darkness, scatter, in the name of Jesus.

PRAYER: I will eat the fruit of my labor, in the name of Jesus.

PRAYER: Today O Lord, visit me as you visited Hannah and take me to the next level, in the name of Jesus.

PRAYER: You that power waiting to attack my blessings, die, in the name of Jesus.

PRAYER: O Lord, let your divine covering be over my children, husband, wife, job, career, business, in the name of Jesus.

PRAYER: Every threat against my life, be nullified, in the name of Jesus.

PRAYER: Every blessing I have lost in the past, be restored double-fold, in the name of Jesus.

PRAYER: Father Lord, take me from where I am to where you want me to be, in the name of Jesus.

PRAYER: You that power delaying my success, die, in the name of Jesus.

PRAYER: Every spirit of sadness hovering over my life, I bind you, in the name of Jesus.

PRAYER: Oil of gladness for favor, locate me now, in the name of Jesus.

PRAYER: Every seed of arrogance in me, be flushed out by the blood of Jesus.

PRAYER: O Lord, baptize me afresh with the spirit of humility, in the name of Jesus.

PRAYER: Lord, I besiege you, send now prosperity, in the name of Jesus.

PRAYER: O God, tonight, disgrace my accusers, in the name of Jesus.

Chapter 4

Prayers for Financial Wisdom

PRAYER: Anything done against my life in the heavenlies, be reversed now, in the name of Jesus.

PRAYER: Any power on evil assignment against my life, kill yourself, in the name of Jesus.

PRAYER: I receive wisdom to fulfill my calling, in the name of Jesus.

PRAYER: Any power anywhere assigned to terminate my life, die, in the name of Jesus.

PRAYER: O Lord, direct me by your word and empower me to eat the fruit therein, in the name of Jesus.

PRAYER: I receive wisdom to understand God's word and affect my generation, in the name of Jesus.

PRAYER: Father Lord, let your angels rub me with your healing balm and make me whole, in the name of Jesus.

PRAYER: Every jinx and spell programmed against my life, break, in the name of Jesus.

PRAYER: Every evil covenant and curses pronounced against my life, break, in the name of Jesus.

PRAYER: Every evil covenant in my foundation, I command you to break, in the name of Jesus.

PRAYER: Every inherited curse and covenant speaking against my prosperity, break by fire, in the name of Jesus.

PRAYER: Anointing for miracles, signs and wonders, come upon my life, in the name of Jesus.

PRAYER: O Lord, let me be celebrated daily, in the name of Jesus.

PRAYER: Every demonic entry into my life, be blocked now, in the name of Jesus.

PRAYER: Father Lord, turn my mourning to dancing,

in the name of Jesus.

PRAYER: Every arrow of bewitchment programmed against my life, destroy your sender, in the name of Jesus.

PRAYER: In the name of Jesus, O Lord, in my time of blessing, change my name forever like Jacob, to the name the devil will never understand.

PRAYER: Angel of restoration, appear, restore my life and heritage, in the name of Jesus.

PRAYER: Every mark of failure in my life, be wiped off, by the blood of Jesus.

PRAYER: You satanic incision in my life, be terminate, by the blood of Jesus.

PRAYER: Oil of success, anoint my head, in the name of Jesus.

PRAYER: Every eater of flesh and drinker of blood threatening to take my life, you time is up, die, in the name of Jesus.

PRAYER: Any power anywhere maneuvering my

blessings, be incapacitated, in the name of Jesus.

PRAYER: Today, let the favor of God locate me, in the name of Jesus.

PRAYER: Wind of prosperity, blow in my direction, in the name of Jesus.

PRAYER: O Lord, order my step, in the name of Jesus.

PRAYER: O Lord, quicken my spirit to be in tune with your Spirit, in the name of Jesus.

PRAYER: My set time of favor shall not be frustrated, in the name of Jesus.

PRAYER: Any demonic thought designed to take me away from the glory of God, be terminated, in the name of Jesus.

PRAYER: I shall prosper in whatever my hands find to do, in the name of Jesus.

PRAYER: Shower of prosperity, rain upon my life, in the name of Jesus.

PRAYER: Every spirit of non-achievement in my life, I bind you, in the name of Jesus.

PRAYER: Every spirit of rejection driving away my opportunities, be cast out, in the name of Jesus.

PRAYER: Grace that attract prosperity, manifest in my life now, in the name of Jesus.

PRAYER: I walk in power, I walk in miracle, I live a life of favor, in the name of Jesus.

PRAYER: From today O Lord, I will prosper in whatsoever I do, in the name of Jesus.

PRAYER: You money, I command you to answer to me, in the name of Jesus.

PRAYER: I refuse to lose my blessings, in the name of Jesus.

PRAYER: Anointing for total restoration and elevation, come upon my life, in the name of Jesus.

PRAYER: Any power using my gifts and glory, die by fire, in the name of Jesus.

PRAYER: O Lord, empower me to fulfill my purpose, in the name of Jesus.

PRAYER: I receive divine mandate to overcome my enemies, in the name of Jesus.

PRAYER: Lord, give me wisdom to recognize my set time of favor, in the name of Jesus.

PRAYER: Let every device of the enemies to be frustrated, in the name of Jesus.

PRAYER: O Lord, let the secret of my enemies be exposed, in the name of Jesus.

PRAYER: Any demonic gate erected against my life, be pulled down, in the name of Jesus.

Chapter 5

Prayers for Total Breakthroughs

PRAYER: O lord, disgrace my enemies and scatter their plans, in the name of Jesus.

PRAYER: Any spiritual wickedness done against my life, be reversed now, in the name of Jesus.

PRAYER: Anointing to overcome powers of darkness, come upon me, in the name of Jesus.

PRAYER: I subdue every ruler of darkness attacking my life, in the name of Jesus.

PRAYER: O Lord, let the truth in your word vindicate me from every evil accusation, in the name of Jesus.

PRAYER: O Lord, set me free in the camp of my enemies and let them be put to shame, in the name of Jesus.

PRAYER: Whatever the devil has stolen from me, killed or destroyed, I recover them back in several-fold, in the name of Jesus.

PRAYER: I receive special anointing to defeat my enemies forever, in the name of Jesus.

PRAYER: I shall be celebrated daily in life, in the name of Jesus.

PRAYER: O Lord, in this mountain, show me your glory and lift me up, in the name of Jesus.

PRAYER: Baptize O Lord with the fullness of the Holy Ghost and let me be divinely directed in all that I do, in the name of Jesus.

PRAYER: I receive power to overcome my enemies daily, in the name of Jesus.

PRAYER: Every hindrance to my breakthroughs, be removed now, in the name of Jesus.

PRAYER: O Lord, do a new thing regarding my life and let it spring up quickly, in the name of Jesus.

211 POWERFUL NIGHT PRAYERS

PRAYER: Anointing to possess my possession, come upon me now, in the name of Jesus.

PRAYER: Father Lord, take me out of every demonic wilderness of life, in the name of Jesus.

PRAYER: Father Lord, create rivers for me in any desert I find myself in life, in the name of Jesus.

PRAYER: Anointing to win life battles and carry on successfully, come upon me now, in the name of Jesus.

PRAYER: Lord Jesus, give me the wisdom I need to rule my generation, in the name of Jesus.

PRAYER: Deliver me from every snare of the enemy, O Lord, in the name of Jesus.

PRAYER: Every divination programmed against my life, break, in the name of Jesus.

PRAYER: Every arrow from the kingdom of darkness attacking my life, I command you to go back to your sender, in the name of Jesus.

PRAYER: Every plan of the wicked be frustrated, in the name of Jesus.

PRAYER: O God, let your fire of deliverance, set me free now, in the name of Jesus.

PRAYER: Anything done against my life and destiny, be nullified, in the name of Jesus.

PRAYER: O Lord, empower me to resist temptations, in the name of Jesus.

PRAYER: You evil arrow from the pit of hell, be destroyed, in the name of Jesus.

PRAYER: Father Lord, deliver me in time of affliction, in the name of Jesus.

PRAYER: Power to escape from every camp of my enemies, I receive you now, in the name of Jesus.

PRAYER: Wherever I am taken captive, Holy Ghost, set me free, in the name of Jesus.

PRAYER: Arise O Lord, let my enemies scatter, in the name of Jesus.

PRAYER: O Lord, shine your light upon my life, in the name of Jesus.

PRAYER: Father Lord, show me your glory, in the name of Jesus.

PRAYER: Any wicked power assigned to cage my life, wherever you are, die by fire, in the name of Jesus.

PRAYER: I refuse to be in any demonic bondage, in the name of Jesus.

PRAYER: No weapon formed against me shall prosper, in the name of Jesus.

PRAYER: Every intention of my enemies, be frustrated, in the name of Jesus.

PRAYER: You that evil tongue lifted against my life, be silenced by fire, in the name of Jesus.

PRAYER: Father Lord, let your holy hammer scatter every demonic weapon designed against my life, in the name of Jesus.

PRAYER: I receive the gift of discernment to detect every bait from the camp of my enemies, in the name of Jesus.

PRAYER: I receive divine power to be focused in life,

in the name of Jesus.

PRAYER: I bind you spirit of confusion, in the name of Jesus.

PRAYER: You that power ministering confusion into my life, I command you to die, in the name of Jesus.

PRAYER: Every principality and power assigned against my life, be terminated, by the blood of Jesus.

PRAYER: Anointing to win all battles in the spiritual ream and physical, overtake my life now, in the name of Jesus.

A Call For Short Review On Amazon

Enjoying this book so far or receiving value from it in anyway? Then, I would like to ask you for a favor: kindly post a quick review for this book on its Amazon page.

When you get to the book page on Amazon, gently scroll down the page till you reach **"Write A Customer Review"** and click on it.

Kindly Click Here to Write the Review Now

BONUS CHAPTERS.

Bonus Chapter 1: Using The Right Tongues When Praying In The Holy Ghost.

Please, join me to thank God for making his strength perfect in weakness through provision of a heavenly tool called *Praying in the Holy Ghost*. God understands that people are weak to connect to him in prayer, due to the numerous hurdles they need to jump before getting their need met. Praying in the Holy Ghost is a powerful resource for tongue speaking Christians. Tongue speaking is a mystery best known to God. Through it, yokes are broken in the spirit realm, burdens are lifted with speed faster than that of lightening, and miracles are made available to those in helpless situation.

It is mandatory that you pray with your spirit and your understanding; sing with your spirit and your understanding (1 Cor 14:14). Understanding that every man has a sin nature, and that there is this tendency of loosing focus while praying, God uniquely provide us with tongue as a sign of Holy Ghost baptism, and tongue as a gift. It is this tongue as a gift that is referred to as the gift of speaking in tongues.

The gift of speaking in tongues can culminate into

diverse kind of tongues and tongues interpretation. With all these assets at your disposal, your faith is optimized when you pray. Moreover, the devil can't understand your desired needs as you communicate them through your spirit to God, and suddenly, you'll become a much sought after achiever soaring high in your pre – designed path of destiny.

Of a truth, our God is awesome. Friend, build up yourselves on your most holy faith, pray in the Holy Ghost (Jude 20).

Use the Right Tongue

Generally speaking, tongues are classified into two, namely; tongue as a sign and tongue as a gift. When speaking in tongues is a sign, the tongues cease after the initial baptism of the Holy Spirit. For a person to continue to speak in tongues, he must receive afterward, tongues as a gift as well as a sign.

Those who receive tongues as a gift can speak in tongues anytime, especially during prayer. The gift of tongues makes possible deep spiritual communications with God, brings progress in one's life of faith. It is a door to deeper prayer and praise, a sign to unbelievers, and also helps to sense devil's plots in advance, and avert them without the knowledge of the tongue speaker.

Bonus Chapter 2: Prayer Pattern To Command Your Breakthroughs.

Observe your prayer in this sequence:

1. **Praise** – Express your love to God by:

By adoration – Praising God for who He is.

Thanksgiving – Make a list of what God has done for you and begin to thank Him.

Praise Him, thank Him and worship Him in songs from the bottom of your heart.

2. **Pray for forgiveness:** Read PS 51. Forgive those who offended you. Then ask God to forgive you all your sins. Ask the blood of Jesus to wash you clean.

3. **Invite Holy Spirit** to direct you, control your utterances. Ask Him to wall off evil attack during your prayer session.

4. **Make your request known;** confess His promises on your needs as stated on the top of the prayer points.

5. **Pray the prayer points** diligently to the end.

6. **Pray for others**, that is, intercede briefly for other people.

7. **Pray against satanic delay** of answer to your prayer.

8. **Thank God** for answered prayer, you may even sing to thank Him.

9. **Recite the grace**

10. **Share** your array of testimonies.

Other Books By the Same Author.

Before proceeding, I will like to thank you for downloading this book. I believe the wisdom in this book will bless your life greatly. Please find below other books that God has orchestrated me write. They are meant to bless your life and family satisfactorily.

Career Change: How To Discover Your Divine Destiny And Total Breakthroughs

21 Keys To Miracle In Helpless Situations: How To Pray When You Can't Pray

Surprise Healing: How to Activate the Miracles in your Spirit

Prayers To Discover your Purpose And How To Start Life Assignment

How To Pray In The Holy Ghost And Win All Battles

Living Beyond Yourself: How To Navigate Into Success And Significance

How To Discover Your Purpose Using 12 Proven Tools

Flight To Purpose: A Step By Step Guide To your Assignment

How To Break The Yoke Of Life - Breaking Curses &

Hindrances

Understanding the Mystery of Destiny

How to Discover Your Life Purpose's Function and Forms

Leadership And Sin Intervention

350 Spiritual Warfare Prayers For Protection, Deliverance And Finances

Relationship Advice – Unplanned Pregnancy: Book 1: The Story, the Pains and the Regrets

Relationship Advice – Unplanned Pregnancy: Book 2: The Avoidable Mistakes during Pregnancy

Relationship Advice – Unplanned Pregnancy: Book 3: Counseling and Recommendations

Spiritual Warfare Prayers Triggered By Prophecy: Powerful Prayer Guide & Prayers for Deliverance, Prosperity & Breakthrough

Miracle Prayer Guide: A Powerful Word of Knowledge Warfare Prayer Approach & Prayers for Protection, Deliverance & Breakthrough

Spiritual Warfare Prayers Wisdom For Success, Healing And Breakthrough

The Prosperity Bible Prayers: 240 Powerful Prayers for

Financial Intelligence and Miracles

Spiritual Warfare Prayers: 230 Prayers for Success and Activating Miracles Of Prayer

Spiritual Warfare Prayers For Blessings And Finances: Over 200 Deliverance and Breakthrough Prayers

Prosperity Prayers: Over 200 Deliverance Prayers for Money, Finances & Favor

Finance & Prosperity: Over 220 Spiritual Warfare Prayers for Divine Favor, Financial Blessings and Money

How To Pray To God For Financial Miracles And Blessings: Over 230 Holy Spirit Inspired Prayers for Deliverance, Breakthrough & Divine Favor

Prayers For Victory In Spiritual Warfare: Over 220 Spiritual Warfare Prayers for Deliverance and Breakthrough

Prayers For Money & Finances: Over 220 Powerful Warfare and Night Prayers for Protection, Financial Prosperity & Intelligence

How to Pray To God For Financial Freedom & Intelligence: Over 300 Powerful Prayers for Release of Detained Blessings, Money & Favor

How to Reposition the Church to the Lord Jesus Christ Standard

<u>The Holy Spirit: Pentecost:</u> An Examination of Today's Christian Living and Doctrine devoid Of Fruits of the Holy Spirit

<u>How to Make Heaven and Have Eternal Life</u>

Let Us Hear from You.

Glad you've been blessed while reading this book.

To connect with the author or feedback, visit:

BLOG: mosesomojola.blogspot.com

E-MAIL: reflects2015@gmail.com

About The Author.

I am the author of the bestseller: "How to discover your divine destiny and total breakthroughs". I spent 16 years working as an Engineer in the Oil and Gas industry before I was divinely conscripted into my divine assignment. I am an author, international speaker, counselor, destiny mentor, business and wellness coach. My specialties are hidden truths, divine assignment, justice, success and leadership.

I run workshops to help people discover their destiny, the unique business God created them to do, how to start and succeed. I also counsel individuals empathetically on issues relating to destiny, employment, health, relationships, and many more, using the awesome power inherent in their destiny, and assist many to become writers and self – publish many books.

EXTRA BONUS PRAYERS: 340 PRAYERS ON FINANCIAL DELIVERANCE AND PROSPERITY

Contents

Preface

Without mincing words, we all at one point or the other are faced with challenges in personal lives and on a global scale, that often threaten to take breathe out of us momentarily. These challenges could come in form of grief, unemployment, illness, divorce, retrogressive relationships, marriage, business, crisis, and the like. And many are confused on how to prevent such occurrence or terminate it as soon as it raises its ugly head. The enemy behind these happenings is the devil, and there is need to handle him in a way that we would not fall prey to his frequent craftiness. This is why this prayer book has been inspirationally written to help you get victory over Satan and his multitudes of demons, and protect, recover and claim your possessions in an uncommon way.

To this end, this book contains more than 340 powerful prayers on deliverance and prosperity. These prayers' divine covering and elevation tentacles include finances, jobs, careers, business, family, relationships, marriage, etc.

The prayers in this book are not meant to be prayed casually, they are highly spiritual. There is no other book like this book. Why? This is because the prayers were released to me by the Holy Spirit for you while meditating on over 120 special scriptures that will help you defeat Satan totally. Friend, As I read each passage, by virtue of my gifts of prophecy and healing, the Holy Spirit instantly released those prayers, and I put them down as I heard the Holy Spirit spoke to my spirit. So you can see clearly that these prayers were not formulated or guessed. This is why I'm fully convinced that this book will be of immense blessings to you.

The prayers in this book covers all areas of your life, you will only be able to appreciate the book when you go through all the prayers. This is because the prayers are spiritually discerned and arranged. You are to pray the prayers in this book with all seriousness. Pray most of them repeatedly before moving to the next prayer. These prayers would be very great during your special midnight prayers. Furthermore, since these prayers were released while meditating on God's word, you can pray this prayer perfectly even if you don't have access to the Holy Bible during your prayer time.

I look forward to your arrays of testimonies as you read this book and add the wisdom and Grace in it to your life and family.

CHAPTER 1

Prayers against Anti-Success Syndrome

PRAYER: O Lord, today, turn my shame to testimonies, in the name of Jesus.

PRAYER: Every challenge in my life, hear the voice of the Lord and be removed forever, in the name of Jesus.

PRAYER: Every traitor in my life, be exposed now, in the name of Jesus.

PRAYER: Every demonic counsel against my life, be frustrated, in the name of Jesus.

PRAYER: O God my Father, increase my faith, in the name of Jesus.

PRAYER: You seed of selfishness in me, die in the name of Jesus.

PRAYER: Every manipulative power assigned against my life to make me love money than my Creator, I command you to die, in the name of Jesus.

PRAYER: You seed of pride in me, die in the name of Jesus.

PRAYER: You my spirit be humble, in the name of Jesus.

PRAYER: Any power anywhere manipulating my blessings, I command you to die, in the name of Jesus.

PRAYER: Any evil altar erected against my inheritance, scatter, in the name of Jesus.

PRAYER: Every eater of flesh and drinker of blood attacking my life, wherever you are, die by fire.

PRAYER: I come out from every demonic bondage

now, in the name of Jesus.

PRAYER: From today O Lord, let my enemies be at peace with me, in the name of Jesus.

PRAYER: Father Lord, let your protection be over me and my family.

PRAYER: You my guarding angel, receive uncommon strength to carry out you assignment.

PRAYER: Holy Spirit, empower me not to offend my guarding angel.

PRAYER: I receive grace to run away from sin.

PRAYER: Holy Spirit strengthen me to keep the Lord's commandment.

PRAYER: I refuse to be slave to money, in the name

of Jesus.

PRAYER: Any altar erected against the will of god for my life, I command you to scatter, in the name of Jesus.

PRAYER: Any strongman programmed to take my life captive, I incapacitate you now, by the blood of Jesus

PRAYER: Fire of deliverance, deliver me from every affliction fashioned against my life, in the name of Jesus.

PRAYER: Every wall of Jericho erected against my fruitfulness, I pull you down, in the name of Jesus.

PRAYER: You my body, soul and spirit, run away from unpardonable sins, in the name of Jesus.

PRAYER: My guarding angel, direct me in the way of the Lord.

PRAYER: I refresh God's covenant of long life upon my life, in the name of Jesus.

PRAYER: Every demonic wall erected against my glory, I pull you down, in the name of Jesus.

PRAYER: Every activity of marine power against my life, be nullified, by the blood of Jesus.

PRAYER: Thou God of vengeance, let your wrath fall upon my accusers.

PRAYER: You spirit of doubt, I bind you, in the name of Jesus.

PRAYER: Lord, give me grace to express the truth at all times.

PRAYER: Father Lord, have mercy upon me and forgive me all my sins.

PRAYER: O Lord, sanctify me again by your Word.

PRAYER: You spirit of greed in my flesh, I bind you now.

PRAYER: O Lord, every sin I have committed that is hindering my life from moving forward, forgive me, in the name of Jesus.

PRAYER: Divine blood of liberation, liberate me from every enchantment and divination, in the name of Jesus.

PRAYER: Every cry of the aggrieved over my life, I silence you now, in the name of Jesus.

PRAYER: Any evil hand raised against my life, wither by fire, in the name of Jesus.

PRAYER: O lord, give me the heart to show mercy to

my persecutors, in the name of Jesus.

PRAYER: O Lord, raise me up to the extent that my enemies will be chocked and beg me for mercy, in the name of Jesus.

PRAYER: O Lord, make me a deliverer like Moses and Joseph, in the name of Jesus.

PRAYER: O Lord, pour upon my life the gift of prophecy, in the name of Jesus.

PRAYER: Anointing to prophesy fall upon my life now, in the name of Jesus.

PRAYER: Father Lord, baptize me afresh with the gift of prophecy, in the name of Jesus.

PRAYER: O God you that made Joseph master rather than slave in the house of Potiphar and in prison, visit me by fire, in the name of Jesus.

PRAYER: Tonight O Lord, let my period in captivity expire, in the name of Jesus.

PRAYER: Anointing that cannot be insulted come upon me now.

PRAYER: Every power anywhere threatening my life, receive the fire of God, in the name of Jesus.

PRAYER: Every evil pit dug against my life, I command it to swallow my enemy, in the name of Jesus.

PRAYER: Wherever I am tied up in the heavenly, angel of deliverance deliver me now, in the name of Jesus.

PRAYER: Lord, let your hand be upon my life, family, business, work, in the name of Jesus.

PRAYER: Holy Spirit renew my strength to do that which I'm divinely designed to do.

PRAYER: You power causing anti-success syndrome in my life, I rebuke you now, in the name of Jesus.

PRAYER: I receive wisdom to pay my tithe regularly, in the name of Jesus.

PRAYER: O Lord, rebuke devourer for my sake, in the name of Jesus.

PRAYER: Father Lord, hence forth, let the Spirit of the Lord Jesus Christ wrap me like a mantle, in the name of Jesus.

PRAYER: O Lord, let the power that descended in the day of Pentecost manifest in my life.

PRAYER: Anointing that cannot be caged, possess me now.

PRAYER: Lord, give me a forerunner to make way for me.

PRAYER: Any power anywhere tampering with my blessings, I command you to die, in the name of Jesus.

PRAYER: Every evil hand place upon my blessings, I command you to wither, in the name of Jesus.

PRAYER: Every serpent of affliction frustrating my intent, I cast you out, in the name of Jesus.

PRAYER: Every spirit of barrenness in my life, I bind you now, in the name of Jesus.

PRAYER: In the name of Jesus, I command every cloud of darkness surrounding my finances, relationships, marriage, business, career, job, work and family to disappear now.

PRAYER: You spirit of miscarriage, I bind you now, in the name of Jesus.

PRAYER: I decree and declare in the name of Jesus, bareness is not my portion.

CHAPTER 2

Prayers Against Evil Foundations Speaking Against

your Fruitfulness

PRAYER: Every channel of reproach in my life, I block you now, in the name of Jesus.

PRAYER: O God, visit me now, and put my mockers to shame, in the name of Jesus.

PRAYER: Every power of darkness speaking against my breakthrough, I silence you now, in the name of Jesus.

PRAYER: O God my father, let my good speak for me in the day of affliction.

PRAYER: In the name of Jesus, over my life, over my family, over my career, business, marriage, I decree and declare, there shall be no loss.

PRAYER: Anything done against my life, be reversed by fire.

PRAYER: Any evil gate erected against my breakthrough, be uprooted now, in the name of Jesus.

PRAYER: O Lord, give me the wisdom to discern every lie of the devil.

PRAYER: O Lord, give me the heart to serve you in spirit and in truth.

PRAYER: Any power anywhere polluting my water of life, die by fire.

PRAYER: Every power making God a liar in my life, die, in the name of Jesus.

PRAYER: I break every inherited curse and covenant, in the name of Jesus.

PRAYER: Every evil foundation speaking against my life, be nullified by the blood of Jesus.

PRAYER: O Lord, empower me to walk humbly with you.

PRAYER: Lord, strength me to demonstrate the love of Christ to anyone I come across irrespective of religion, in the name of Jesus.

PRAYER: I receive wisdom that surpasses that of Solomon, in the name of Jesus.

PRAYER: Father Lord, give me understanding heart.

PRAYER: You seed of greed in me, die, in the name of Jesus.

PRAYER: O Lord, give me the wisdom to fear you in all my dealings with men.

PRAYER: Any power anywhere dragging my blessings with me, I command you to die, in the name of Jesus.

PRAYER: In the name of Jesus, you my spirit, discern and reject any wisdom from the devil meant to destroy me, in the name of Jesus.

PRAYER: O Lord, give me the grace to know the wisdom in every matter brought before me.

PRAYER: Father Lord, give me the kind of wisdom that will open flood gate of favor upon my life.

PRAYER: Every seed of wickedness in me, die, in the name of Jesus.

PRAYER: Spirit of service and humility, take over my life.

PRAYER: O Lord, give me the heart to serve you with

fear and trembling.

PRAYER: Lord Jesus, give me the heart to endure where I need to endure in life and quit when I need to quit without losing my blessings.

PRAYER: Any power anywhere assigned to take me away from the glory of God, I command you to die, in Jesus' name.

PRAYER: I receive grace to keep the Lord's commandment, in the name of Jesus.

PRAYER: Any power anywhere assigned to curse me, be frustrated, in the name of Jesus.

PRAYER: Every curse pronounced against my life, I nullify you, by the blood of Jesus.

PRAYER: Thou Spirit of obedience from the throne of grace, take over my life now, in the name of Jesus.

PRAYER: Anointing to live in holiness, possess me now.

PRAYER: Satan, I rebuke you, get behind me, in the name of Jesus.

PRAYER: You spirit of covetousness, I bind you, in the name of Jesus.

PRAYER: I receive grace to live in faith and obedience to God all the days of my life.

PRAYER: You spirit of poverty programmed against my life, I cast you out now, in the name of Jesus.

PRAYER: Father Lord, give me grace to fulfill the number of my days, in the name of Jesus.

PRAYER: I refuse to die young.

PRAYER: Every cry of the aggrieved over my life, I silence you in the name of Jesus.

PRAYER: Anointing that cannot be insulted, come upon my life.

PRAYER: Every evil arrow programmed against my life, go back to your sender.

PRAYER: O Lord give me the wisdom I need to claim my blessings.

PRAYER: Father Lord, give me the heart to serve you the way you want me to.

PRAYER: Lord, let your strong hand be upon me anywhere I go.

PRAYER: Wherever I am O Lord, let the kingship in me manifest, in the name of Jesus.

PRAYER: Anointing for success and all-round breakthroughs, come upon my life.

PRAYER: Holy Spirit, help me to build integrity and hold on to my Maker.

PRAYER: O God my father, give me the unction to function in life and ministry.

PRAYER: O Lord, give me that subordinate that will rightly assist me to fulfill my life mission.

PRAYER: Every power assigned to take me back to Egypt, die, in the name of Jesus.

PRAYER: Every spirit of doubt concerning my calling, I bind you now.

PRAYER: Lord, give me the wisdom to follow you to the end.

PRAYER: O God, tonight let your angels ascend and descend and take me to my promise land, in the name of Jesus.

PRAYER: Every evil seed planted into my life that is luring me into sin, I command you to die, in the name of Jesus.

PRAYER: Father Lord, empower me afresh to live a holy life.

PRAYER: Every seed of covetousness in me, die, in the name of Jesus.

PRAYER: Every spirit of deceit in me, I bind you, in the name of Jesus.

PRAYER: Holy Spirit, empower me to place money in its right perspective.

PRAYER: You spirit of lust of the flesh, lust of the eyes and pride of life, I bind you in the name of Jesus.

PRAYER: You the spirit envy and jealousy dwelling in my flesh, I cast you out in the name of Jesus.

PRAYER: I refuse to be foolish with money and investment, in the name of Jesus.

PRAYER: You demonic spirit behind love of money, I rebuke you, in the name of Jesus.

PRAYER: In any way the devil has crafted to tempt me through money, I nullify it now, by the blood of Jesus.

CHAPTER 3

Prayers Against Evil Diversion of Blessings

PRAYER: You the seed of hatred flourishing in my flesh, die, in the name of Jesus.

PRAYER: Every demon standing at the gate of my prosperity, I bind you, in the name of Jesus.

PRAYER: O Lord, give me the heart and wisdom to serve my generation.

PRAYER: Every cloud of darkness surrounding my prosperity, disappear, in the name of Jesus.

PRAYER: O Lord, let your light shine in the camp of my enemies and all my snatched blessings be returned unto me, in the name of Jesus.

PRAYER: Holy Spirit, strengthen me to trust the Lord the way He want me to trust Him.

PRAYER: Every spirit of worldliness in me, I bind you now, in the name of Jesus.

PRAYER: Every power tormenting my destiny, die, in the name of Jesus.

PRAYER: Today O Lord, wear me your garment of glory, in the name of Jesus.

PRAYER: Every bitterness in my foundation, I terminate you now, in the name of Jesus.

PRAYER: every occultic gathering against my divine wealth, scatter, in the name of Jesus.

PRAYER: O Lord, exempt me from destruction of any kind, in the name of Jesus.

PRAYER: Father Lord, frustrate the intent of the enemies concerning my life.

PRAYER: Every mark of affliction in my life, I wipe you off by the blood of Jesus.

PRAYER: Every evil cord used to tie my blessings, I cut you off by the sword of God.

PRAYER: Any power denying me my joy, be frustrated, in the name of Jesus.

PRAYER: Anything in me diverting the blessings of God from manifesting in my life, I flush you out by the blood of Jesus.

PRAYER: Any evil wind blowing against my prosperity, I command you to cease, in the name of Jesus.

PRAYER: Every power causing failure at the edge of my breakthrough, I command you to die, in the name of Jesus.

PRAYER: You anti-success syndrome, I terminate you now, by the power of God.

PRAYER: You spirit of confusion surrounding my life assignment, I cast you out, in the name of Jesus.

PRAYER: O God, arise, show me your glory, in the name of Jesus.

PRAYER: Every cloud covering my star, disappear now, in the name of Jesus.

PRAYER: Father Lord, make me a king in the land of my affliction that your name may be glorified, in the name of Jesus.

PRAYER: every seed of sadness in me, die, in the name of Jesus.

PRAYER: Holy Spirit empower me to resist

temptation, in the name of Jesus.

PRAYER: O Lord, baptize me afresh with the grace to build my integrity and be above board, in the name of Jesus.

PRAYER: Let every evil plan against me turn to breakthroughs, in the name of Jesus.

PRAYER: By your power O Lord, let my mockers be the mock, in the name of Jesus.

PRAYER: You my spirit be submissive to the Holy spirit, in the name of Jesus.

PRAYER: You reproach in my life, your time has expired, die in the name of Jesus.

PRAYER: Every demonic gang up against me, I command you to scatter, in the name of Jesus.

PRAYER: O God, turn the wisdom of my enemy to foolishness, in the name of Jesus.

PRAYER: The Lord will fight for me and I shall hold my peace, in the name of Jesus.

PRAYER: The Lord comforts me on every side from today, in the name of Jesus.

PRAYER: O lord, put your fear in the heart of my enemies.

PRAYER: Divine sword of deliverance, fight for me in the camp of my enemies.

PRAYER: Every evil altar taking my life captive, release me and die.

PRAYER: Every monitoring spirit assigned against my life, I bind you now.

PRAYER: Arise O Lord, let your enemies, my enemies scatter, in the name of Jesus.

PRAYER: I receive grace to overcome every snare of the enemy, in the name of Jesus.

PRAYER: Spirit of holiness, take over my life, in the name of Jesus.

PRAYER: O Lord, sanctify my thought.

PRAYER: Lord, give me wisdom to discern good and bad.

PRAYER: Holy Spirit, choose my friends for me.

PRAYER: Every power ministering confusion into my life and family, die, in the name of Jesus.

PRAYER: Every arrow of sorrow from the camp of

my enemies programmed against my life, I command you to go back to your sender, in the name of Jesus.

PRAYER: I refused to be wasted, in the name of Jesus.

PRAYER: Any power assigned to pollute my goodwill, die, in the name of Jesus

PRAYER: In the name of Jesus, I command every bitterness in my life to turn to sweetness.

PRAYER: Any evil seed cohabiting with my blessing, I uproot you by fire.

PRAYER: Lord, give me the grace to follow your will for my life.

PRAYER: O Lord, change my name to the name the devil will not understand.

PRAYER: Every affliction from the kingdom of darkness over my life, catch fire, in the name of Jesus.

PRAYER: Thou fire of deliverance, come upon my life.

PRAYER: Every trick of the devil against my life, be exposed now, in the name of Jesus.

PRAYER: You spirit of selfishness operating in my life, I bind you now, in the name of Jesus.

PRAYER: In the name of Jesus, I bind every serpent of affliction troubling my life.

PRAYER: Lord Jesus, give me the heart to serve you.

PRAYER: I receive divine power to resist and overcome temptation.

PRAYER: Every power programmed to mock my calling, be disgraced by fire.

PRAYER: You spirit of error, I bind you, in the name of Jesus.

PRAYER: You power of the grave fashioned against my life, I command you to die.

PRAYER: Any evil power designed to take me away from the palace, wherever you are, die, in the name of Jesus.

PRAYER: Father Lord, preserve my life in time of affliction and give me victory.

PRAYER: You spirit of slavery and rejection, I bind you in the name of Jesus.

PRAYER: You spirit of Jezebel assigned against my life, I cast you out, in the name of Jesus.

PRAYER: Any power anywhere assigned to pull me down, be disgraced by fire.

PRAYER: O Lord, renew my strength and shame my accusers.

PRAYER: Divine health is my heritage, I claim it now, in the name of Jesus.

PRAYER: O Lord, let the love for you manifest in anything I do in life.

PRAYER: Every sorrow in my life, be terminated, in the name of Jesus.

PRAYER: Every arrow from the camp of my enemy designed to make me weep, I command you to go back to your sender.

PRAYER: Tonight O Lord, deliver me from every

shadow of death.

CHAPTER 4

Prayers Against Serpent of Affliction attacking Any Area of your Life

PRAYER: O lord, strengthen me in my weakness.

PRAYER: Divine Ministering spirits and flame of fire, appear and fight for me in my unconsciousness, and give me victory.

PRAYER: Let anointing that break every demonic yoke, come upon my life, in the name of Jesus.

PRAYER: Thou sword of vengeance, locate the camp of my enemies and crush them to pieces.

PRAYER: Every enchantment and divination programmed against my life, I command you to break, in the name of Jesus.

PRAYER: You wandering spirit fashioned against my

life, I bind you now.

PRAYER: Any power anywhere that sold me into slavery, release me, restore me and die, in the name of Jesus.

PRAYER: Any power manipulating my finances, die, in the name of Jesus.

PRAYER: Any power taking my marriage, children, wife, husband, work, career, job, business, investment captive, release them and die, in the name of Jesus.

PRAYER: Any power anywhere making God a liar concerning His promises in my life, be disgraced tonight by fire, in the name of Jesus.

PRAYER: I receive sound wisdom and knowledge to handle every life issue, in the name of Jesus.

PRAYER: Holy Spirit, discipline me to be obedient to

God's Word.

PRAYER: O God, teach me to know your will.

PRAYER: You garment of poverty, I burn you to ashes, in the name of Jesus.

PRAYER: I receive power, spirit of love and sound mind, in the name of Jesus.

PRAYER: From today, I decree and declare that my struggles in life are over, in the name of Jesus.

PRAYER: You weed or tare sowed in my vineyard by the enemy, I command you to be uprooted, in the name of Jesus.

PRAYER: Spirit of patience and perseverance possess me now.

PRAYER: Spirit of error and fatal mistakes, I bind you now, in the name of Jesus.

PRAYER: I refuse to die before my time, in the name of Jesus.

PRAYER: Father Lord, refresh my strength to serve you better.

PRAYER: I refuse to suffer in vain, in the name of Jesus.

PRAYER: Every plot against my finances, work, business and marriage, I command you to scatter, in the name of Jesus.

PRAYER: Every spirit of timidity, I bind you now, in the name of Jesus.

PRAYER: Holy Spirit help me to grow in the word of God daily and meditate therein.

PRAYER: Father Lord, by your mercy, rebuke devourer for my sake.

PRAYER: Holy Spirit, empower me to live a holy life.

PRAYER: O Lord, sanctify me by your word.

PRAYER: I receive grace and strength to live a righteous life, in the name of Jesus.

PRAYER: You seed of unforgiveness in me, die, in the name of Jesus.

PRAYER: You my life, be subjected to the Holy spirit, in the name of Jesus.

PRAYER: Every demonic bait of the world, I reject you by the blood of Jesus, and refuse to become prey, in the name of Jesus.

PRAYER: Power from above to live a holy life and fear God in all that I do, come upon my life now, in the name of Jesus.

PRAYER: O Lord, my times are in your hand, preserve my life and let me see my children children, in the name of Jesus.

PRAYER: Father Lord, let the good that I do, not be used against me in the evil world, in the name of Jesus.

PRAYER: Anointing for divine service, come upon my life, in the name of Jesus.

PRAYER: O Lord, give me the heart to demonstrate servant leadership.

PRAYER: Every spirit of pride in me, I bind you, in the name of Jesus.

PRAYER: O Lord, today, turn the wisdom of my

oppressors to foolishness, in the name of Jesus.

PRAYER: Every covenant of bareness in my life, break, in the name of Jesus.

PRAYER: Thou fire of deliverance, come upon my life, in the name of Jesus.

PRAYER: The grace to grow in the things of God, I receive it now, in the name of Jesus.

PRAYER: Any power using my glory in the demonic world, I command you to release it to me now and die, in the name of Jesus.

PRAYER: O Lord, anything I have lost to the kingdom of darkness, restore them to me now, in the name of Jesus.

PRAYER: Any power assigned to make me forget my divine assignment, die, in the name of Jesus.

PRAYER: O Lord, comfort me and let me be at rest on every side, in the name of Jesus.

PRAYER: Every spirit of barrenness programmed against my life, I cast you out, in the name of Jesus.

PRAYER: Any evil seed programmed into my life, I flush you out by the blood of Jesus.

PRAYER: Any power anywhere assigned to mock my destiny, I command you to die, in the name of Jesus.

PRAYER: Every power of limitation programmed into my life, I render you impotent, in the name of Jesus.

PRAYER: I come out of every demonic cage now, in Jesus' name.

PRAYER: You that power caging my glory, be frustrated, in the name of Jesus.

PRAYER: Anything in my life hindering the glory of god from manifesting, I command you to come out, in the name of Jesus.

PRAYER: O God my father, empower me afresh to be holy.

PRAYER: Every seed of pride in me, die, in the name of Jesus.

PRAYER: Thou spirit of humility from the throne of grace, possess me now.

CHAPTER 5

Prayers for Power and Wisdom to Handle Life Issues

PRAYER: O Lord, help me to resist temptation.

PRAYER: Every evil conspiracy against my life, scatter, in the name of Jesus.

PRAYER: O Lord, let every evil counsel likened to the counsel of Ahitophel be turned to foolishness, in the name of Jesus.

PRAYER: Arise O Lord, let my enemies scatter.

PRAYER: Tonight O Lord, let all my enemies be put to shame, in the name of Jesus.

PRAYER: Thou God that delivered Daniel in the Lion's den, deliver me now from every form of affliction, in the name of Jesus.

PRAYER: Every demonic gang up against my life, scatter, in the name of Jesus.

PRAYER: Father Lord, put confusion in the camp of my enemies.

PRAYER: Any evil arrow fashioned against my life, go back to your sender, in the name of Jesus.

PRAYER: You my destiny, speak by fire.

PRAYER: Every power ministering confusion over my calling and life purpose, die, in the name of Jesus.

PRAYER: Every yoke of slavery placed upon my life, break, in the name of Jesus.

PRAYER: Holy Spirit, help me tame my tongue.

PRAYER: O Lord, empower me to love others as myself.

PRAYER: O Lord, baptize me afresh with the spirit of faithfulness and meekness, in the name of Jesus.

PRAYER: O Lord, give me the heart to serve you like David.

PRAYER: Every serpent of affliction troubling my relationships and my marriage, catch fire, in the name of Jesus.

PRAYER: You yoke of bareness, I break you now, in the name of Jesus.

PRAYER: I refuse to die young, in the name of Jesus.

PRAYER: I shall not die but live and declare the works of the Lord

PRAYER: Any power splitting my blessing, be frustrated now, in the name of Jesus.

PRAYER: I command every agenda of the wicked to be frustrated now, in the name of Jesus.

PRAYER: As the Lord liveth, today, I command every siege placed upon my life to be lifted now, in Jesus' name.

PRAYER: Every power programming bitterness into my life, I command you to die.

PRAYER: Every evil pronouncement against my life, I terminate you now, by the blood of Jesus.

PRAYER: Thou blood of sprinkling that speaketh better things than the blood of Abel, speak on my behalf against any demonic altar working against my life.

PRAYER: O God my Father, protect me and family from the hands of the evil ones.

PRAYER: Father Lord, let your angels fight every seen and unseen battle for me and give me victory.

PRAYER: Increase my faith, O Lord, in the name of Jesus.

PRAYER: Every seed of selfishness and greed embedded in my flesh. Die, in the name of Jesus.

PRAYER: Father Lord; give me strength in time of weakness.

PRAYER: Today O Lord, put confusion in the camp of my enemies and give me victory.

PRAYER: Any power anywhere speaking against the will of God over my life, I command you to die, in the name of Jesus.

PRAYER: O Lord, sanctify my mouth to speak only those things that will glorify your name.

PRAYER: I silence every whisper from the devil, in the name of Jesus.

PRAYER: I command every word that comes out of my mouth to bless my body, soul and spirit in righteousness, in the name of Jesus.

PRAYER: O Lord, be merciful to me every day of my life.

PRAYER: Holy Spirit, give me the wisdom to make God first in whatever I do in life.

PRAYER: You my delayed blessings, wherever you've been held captive, be released by fire, in the name of Jesus.

PRAYER: Any power in the heavenly working against my life, what are you waiting for? Die, in the name of Jesus.

PRAYER: Every garment of shame and reproach in my life, catch fire, in the name of Jesus.

PRAYER: Every long battle in my life, be defeated today, in the name of Jesus.

PRAYER: Any power holding my life in bondage, die by fire.

PRAYER: Any power ministering confusion into my life, career, work, business, marriage, relationships, I command you to die, in the name of Jesus.

PRAYER: Today, I come out of every reproach, in the name of Jesus.

PRAYER: I receive strength to operate in the

atmosphere of love, in the name of Jesus.

PRAYER: Thou fire of deliverance, set me free from every oppression of the enemy, in the name of Jesus.

PRAYER: Every serpent of affliction hindering my blessings from manifesting, I incapacitate you now, in the name of Jesus.

PRAYER: Every aggression of the enemy against my life, I terminate you by the blood of Jesus.

PRAYER: Thou power of resurrection, visit me today and purge out every garbage in my life.

PRAYER: O Lord, give me the heart to serve you in spirit and in truth.

PRAYER: Any power polluting my zeal for God, catch fire.

PRAYER: O Lord, let the boldness that came upon Joshua and Caleb, come upon my life now, in the name of Jesus.

PRAYER: Father Lord, silence my accusers, in the name of Jesus.

PRAYER: Every demonic gang up against my life, scatter, in the name of Jesus.

PRAYER: Thou sword of vengeance, attack my enemies and tear them into pieces, in the name of Jesus.

PRAYER: Holy Spirit, in the day affliction and persecution, work through me and speak through me so that God's name will be glorified, in the name of Jesus.

PRAYER: You my destiny, speak for me in time of affliction.

PRAYER: Father Lord, baptize me afresh with the spirit of humility to recognize you as my source.

PRAYER: You seed of covetousness flourishing in my life, I command you to die, in the name of Jesus.

PRAYER: You spirit of greed in my life, I bind you now, in the name of Jesus.

PRAYER: You spirit of worry, I bind you, in the name of Jesus.

A Call For Short Review On Amazon

Enjoying this book so far or receiving value from it in anyway? Then, I would like to ask you for a favor: kindly post a quick review for this book on its Amazon page.

When you get to the book page on Amazon, gently scroll down the page till you reach **"Write A Customer Review"** and click on it.

Kindly Click Here to Write the Review Now

Printed in Great Britain
by Amazon